Self-trust is the first
secret of success.

Ralph Waldo Emerson

Blue Mountain Arts®
Other books in the *Shapes of Life*™ series...

Daughters

Friendship

Girlfriends

Great Teachers

Love

Marriage

Mothers

Parenting

Sisters

Sons

Words for Teenagers

*Believe &
Succeed*

A Blue Mountain Arts® Collection
to Inspire Success by
Believing in Yourself and Your Dreams

Edited by Patricia Wayant

Blue Mountain Press ™

Boulder, Colorado

We wish to thank Susan Polis Schutz for permission to reprint the following poem
that appears in this publication: "Always Listen to Your Own Heart." Copyright ©
1983 by Stephen Schutz and Susan Polis Schutz. All rights reserved.

Library of Congress Control Number: 2004094588
ISBN: 0-88396-878-9

ACKNOWLEDGMENTS appear at end of book.

Certain trademarks are used under license.
BLUE MOUNTAIN PRESS is registered in U.S. Patent and Trademark Office.

Manufactured in Thailand.
First Printing: 2004

 This book is printed on recycled paper.

Blue Mountain Arts, Inc.

P.O. Box 4549, Boulder, Colorado 80306

Contents

(Authors listed in order of first appearance)

Believe that
You Can,
and
You Will...

When you come to believe in all
that you are and all that you can become,
there will be no cause for doubt.
Believe in your heart, for it offers hope.
Believe in your mind, for it offers direction.
Believe in your soul, for it offers strength.
But above all else... believe in yourself.

Leslie Neilson

When you believe you can,
the world opens up to you
in so many marvelous ways...
The sun shines brighter,
opportunities become steppingstones
to future achievements,
and all those dreams you've tucked away
suddenly seem worth reaching for.
As one door closes, another one opens,
and you have the optimism
to walk through it and
give it your best.
Suddenly, difficulties aren't so devastating
because they are viewed as
opportunities to build your strength.

With each step you take,
another lesson is learned,
and with each mistake you make,
growth is achieved.
When you believe you can,
you'll discover that even though the world
may not always be easy,
faith can lift you above the rushing tides
and give you wings
you never knew you had.
So believe, and fly!

★ Linda C. Grazulis

Always bear in mind that your own resolution to success is more important than any other one thing.

Abraham Lincoln

Fifteen Things
Everyone Should Do

Believe in yourself.
Be the miracle you are.
Let all the wonder in.
Let all the worries out.

Follow your heart.
Trust your instincts.
Listen to the song that sings in you.
Let your spirit dance to that tune.

Reach down deep and search within.
Discover how strong you can be.
Rise up as high as a wishing star.
Love the possibilities you see.

Remember: it's all about choices.
Realize: the decisions are up to you.
And don't forget:
    you're in the driver's seat,
    and you can travel through life
      in any direction you choose.

 Douglas Pagels

You control your destiny, and having faith in yourself controls how far you can go.

Look into your heart, search your dreams, and be honest about what you really want; then do whatever it takes to get it.

Live like you mean it. Believe you can… and you will!

Barbara Cage

The Road to Success Begins with a Single Thought: "I Think I Can"

All successful achievement
has come from a single thought:
I think I can.
In life we help create
our own triumphs and defeats,
depending on how and what
we think.

The mind is a very powerful thing,
and by listening to our thoughts
we are able to tap into
the unlimited power
    it has to offer.

★ Milton Willis and Michael Willis

✶ Aim High
and
Reach for
the Sky

We must never be afraid to go too far,
for success lies just beyond.

Marcel Proust

Listen to that voice inside you
that says you can accomplish anything.

Trust that feeling that tells you
you can achieve all that you hope for.

Believe that everything you want
is waiting for you.

Hold on to the knowledge
that nothing is impossible.

Remember that each person
who has ever achieved a goal
started out with only a dream.

 Jason Blume

Always aim higher than
you believe you can reach.
So often, you'll discover
that when your talents
are set free by your
imagination, you can
achieve any goal.

Edmund O'Neill

No matter what you do, throw yourself into it wholeheartedly. The more of yourself you invest, the more you'll reap the benefits.

★ Donna Gephart

Be an adventurer. Stake out the new frontier instead of clinging to the old and familiar. Let your pioneer spirit keep you moving forward. Visit new territories, learn new skills, and meet new people.

★ Jacqueline Schiff

Be not afraid of greatness.

★ William Shakespeare

You Can Be
or Do Anything!

Imagine yourself to be the type of person you want to be, and then be it. You may have to let go of some bad habits and develop some more positive ones, but don't give up — for it is only in trying and persisting that dreams come true.

Expect changes to occur, and realize that the power to make those changes comes from within you. Your thoughts and actions, the way you spend your time, your choices and decisions determine who you are and who you will become.

You are capable and worthy of being and doing anything. You just need the discipline and determination to see it through. It won't come instantly, and you may backslide from time to time, but don't let that deter you. Never give up.

Life is an ever-changing process, and nothing is final. Therefore, each moment and every new day is a chance to begin anew and see your wishes and dreams come true.

 Barbara Cage

What Is Success?

Each person has his own idea of
what success would mean.... To some
persons, success means fame; to some,
it means fortune in money; to others
it means only love and happiness.

Asa Bushnell Zu Tavern

Success is never settling for less than
all that you can be. It's taking the
high road when you could play it safe
by staying on that old familiar path.

Success is seeing with your heart,
moving to the beat of inspiration,
listening to your dreams,
and holding every hope before you,
like a banner waving in the sky
offering you a place among the stars.

Success is never giving up
because you know in your heart
that being all you can
is where you want to be.

 Barbara J. Hall

The man is a success who has lived
well, laughed often, and loved much;
who has gained the respect of intelligent
men and the love of children; who has
filled his niche and accomplished his
task; who leaves the world better than
he found it, whether by an improved
poppy, a perfect poem, or a rescued soul;
who never lacked appreciation of earth's
beauty or failed to express it; who
looked for the best in others and gave
the best he had.

Robert Louis Balfour Stevenson

Success is...
striving to reach your objective,
as hard and strenuous as it may seem;
conquering a challenge
when so much time
is involved.

Success is...
taking a chance and realizing
you can achieve the things you dream of;
finding that your wishes
are strong deep inside you.

Success is...
believing in your abilities;
knowing that you have the strength,
determination, and willpower
to accomplish your goals.

 Lynne Fadden

Success is a reflection...
 of all the recognition you deserve,
all the determination that
 lights your path,
and all the wisdom that guides
 your steps.

       Douglas Pagels

Success is doing whatever puts the twinkle in your eye, the melody in your heart, the pretty in your smile, and the sunny in your sky...

It's whatever keeps the good in your friendships, gives you endless opportunities, brings you positive experiences, allows you to recall the sweetest memories, and makes you thankful for your blessings...

It's whatever helps you to find answers to your prayers, health for your body, satisfaction in your soul, commitment to what's important, and joy in each new day...

It's love... love in your heart, love in your life, and the love that inspires your dreams to come true.

 Donna Fargo

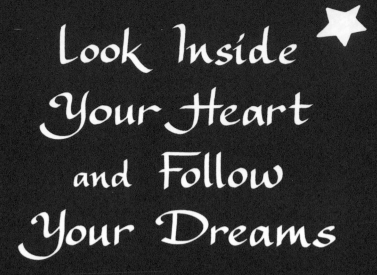

Look Inside Your Heart and Follow Your Dreams

As long as you are true to the strength within your own heart... you can never go wrong.

Ashley Rice

Be true to your dreams, and keep them alive. Never let anyone change your mind about what you feel you can achieve.

Be true to the light that is deep within you. Hold on to your faith, hope, and joy for life. Keep good thoughts in your mind and good feelings in your heart.

Be true to yourself in the paths that you choose. Follow your talents and passions. Don't take the roads others say you must follow; take the ones that will keep your spirits alive with enthusiasm and everlasting joy.

Most of all, never forget that there is no brighter light than the one within you. Follow that inner light to your own personal greatness.

⭐ Jacqueline Schiff

Always Listen to Your Own Heart

You cannot listen
to what others
want you to do
You must listen
to yourself
Society
family
friends
and loved ones
do not know what
you must do
Only you know
and only you
can do what is
right for you

So start right now
You will need to
work very hard
You will need to
overcome many obstacles
You will need to go
against the better
judgment of some people
and you will need to
bypass their prejudices
But you can have
whatever you want
if you try hard enough

So start right now and
you will live
a life designed
by you and
for you
and you will
love
your
life

 Susan Polis Schutz

D̲o̲ your work with a whole heart and you will succeed.

Elbert Hubbard

Every goal that has ever been reached
began with just one step —
and the belief that it could be attained.
Dreams really can come true
but they are most often the result
of hard work, determination,
    and persistence.

When the end of the journey
seems impossible to reach,
remember that all you need to do
is take one more step.
Stay focused on your goal
and remember...
each small step will bring you
    a little closer.

When the road becomes hard to travel
and it feels as if you'll never reach the end...
look deep inside your heart
and you will find strength
    you never knew you had.

 Jason Blume

Don't Give Up

There may be times when you want to give up, but don't listen to the voice of doubt. Stay strong and remind yourself that you can do anything.

Rachyl Taylor

There have been many times
In my own life
When I have wanted to give up
But I wouldn't let myself
And nor should you

There is nothing you can't do
You can be anything you want to be
Believe in yourself
Like others believe in you

If you try ten times and you fail
Then do it eleven times
Never believe in the words "I can't"
You can... and you will

★ Susan J. Kievitt

I do not think there is any other quality so essential to success of any kind as the quality of perseverance.

John Davidson Rockefeller, Sr.

Have faith in your ability
to meet obstacles head on
and climb the mountain
to the summit of success.

Have faith in your ability
to rise above disappointments
    and even failures,
and prove the truth
that nothing is impossible.

Have faith in your ability
to stand tall and unshakable
though the odds are stacked
    against you.

Never give up or give in,
even when doubts and fears
threaten to rob you of
    a victory.

Hang on to hope;
strive for success;
reach for the stars and beyond;
never give up.

Have faith in yourself
    and your abilities!

★ Linda Mooneyham

Many of life's failures are people who did not realize how close they were to success when they gave up.

Thomas Alva Edison

People who succeed don't give up.
When life gets rough, they hang in
until the going gets better.
They are flexible.
They realize there is more than one way
and are willing to try others.
They know they are not perfect.
They respect their weaknesses
while making the most of their strengths.
They fall, but they don't stay down.
They stubbornly refuse to let a fall
    keep them from climbing.

People who succeed don't blame
    fate for their failures
nor luck for their successes.
They accept responsibility for their lives.
They are positive thinkers
who see good in all things.
From the ordinary, they make the extraordinary.
They believe in the path they have chosen
even when it's hard, even when others
can't see where they are going.
They are patient.
They know a goal is only as worthy
as the effort that's required to achieve it.

 Nancye Sims

Hold On to Your Dreams

It takes a strong person
to commit to a dream,
to give it time to grow and come to life.
It takes hard work and sacrifice,
dedication and resolve,
to work through bumps in the road
and stumbling blocks that stand in the way.
It may be difficult, but you can do it.
Don't let anything discourage you.
You are strong and capable enough
to believe that happiness lies ahead.
The future rests in your hands.
Only you can take your dream
and turn it into a reality.
You are capable of making
your brightest dreams come true.
No matter what you do,
you hold the key
that can open doors to your future.

Hold your dreams close to your heart
and strive to make them come true.
Realize that it will not always be easy —
sometimes you may feel like giving up —
but remember that you are strong.
Value the hard times you experience
because they help to make you stronger.
Look forward to the day when
your brightest dreams will come true.
Have faith in yourself,
be strong, and hold on.
Keep believing in yourself,
because dreams are treasures
that grow from the heart.

 Shannon M. Lester

The Special Feeling of Success...

There is only one success —
to be able to spend your life
in your own way.

Christopher Morley

Great achievers are those who
follow the yearning of their souls.
They are those who challenge themselves
with daily sacrifices
and relentlessly endure the
inconveniences and consequences
that occur as a result of their goals.
They are focused on developing themselves,
mastering their unique abilities,
and making their dreams a part
of their lifestyles.
They create their own lives
by never wasting a single day
and possessing the inner strength
to carry on through all of life's changes
with an open mind
and a hopeful heart.

★ Deanna Beisser

The reward of a thing well done is
to have done it.

Ralph Waldo Emerson

When you give each day
  all you can...
when you fill every day
  with substance...
when each day is a steppingstone
  toward your goal...
You are rewarded for all
your hard work and determination,
and you should feel proud of yourself
  and what you've accomplished.

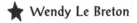 Wendy Le Breton

Joyous people are not only the happiest, but the longest lived, the most useful, and the most successful.

O. S. Marden

Sometimes in this world,
we measure success
by looking at material things —
and we hope that someday
we will have all
we could ever hope for.
But the kind of success
you can really be proud of
is knowing that,
in addition to your abilities
    and determination,
you have a kind, giving heart,
and you are a gentle, caring,
    and loving person.
That's a rare combination.
It shines through,
and it will lead you
to all the success —
    and all the happiness —
you deserve.

— Jason Blume

There's nothing as sweet
as the sound of success,
and nothing as wonderful
as a dream celebrated and shared.
May you continue to follow your heart and
become the very best that you can be.

Linda E. Knight

May your accomplishments cause you to reflect on what a gift your life is to yourself and to others. The competition in the world is so great today, and every goal reached is something to be proud of. When all the elements come together to gain someone recognition, it is truly something to be thankful for.

May your achievements inspire you to continue to do the things that are important to you and that will help you to keep on making your dreams come true. I hope the pride others have in you will encourage you to be all that you desire to be.

May your tomorrows hold new beginnings for you, and may your future be bright. May the joy of every lesson learned and every goal reached advance your feeling of fulfillment and keep you on a positive path.

 Donna Fargo

ACKNOWLEDGMENTS

We gratefully acknowledge the permission granted by the following authors and authors' representatives to reprint poems or excerpts from their publications.

Linda C. Grazulis for "When you believe you can...." Copyright © 2004 by Linda C. Grazulis. All rights reserved.

Milton Willis and Michael Willis for "The Road to Success Begins with a Single Thought." Copyright © 2004 by Milton Willis and Michael Willis. All rights reserved.

Jason Blume for "Listen to that voice inside you," "Every goal that has ever been reached," and "Sometimes in this world...." Copyright © 2004 by Jason Blume. All rights reserved.

Jacqueline Schiff for "Be an adventurer." Copyright © 2004 by Jacqueline Schiff. All rights reserved.

Barbara J. Hall for "Success is never settling for less...." Copyright © 2004 by Barbara J. Hall. All rights reserved.

Lynne Fadden for "Success is...." Copyright © 2004 by Lynne Fadden. All rights reserved.

PrimaDonna Entertainment Corp. for "Success is doing whatever..." and "May your accomplishments..." by Donna Fargo. Copyright © 2004 by PrimaDonna Entertainment Corp. All rights reserved.

Susan J. Kievitt for "There have been many times...." Copyright © 2004 by Susan J. Kievitt. All rights reserved.

Linda Mooneyham for "Have faith in your ability...." Copyright © 2004 by Linda Mooneyham. All rights reserved.

Shannon M. Lester for "Hold On to Your Dreams." Copyright © 2004 by Shannon M. Lester. All rights reserved.

Deanna Beisser for "Great achievers are those who...." Copyright © 2004 by Deanna Beisser. All rights reserved.

Wendy Le Breton for "When you give each day...." Copyright © 2004 by Wendy Le Breton. All rights reserved.

Linda E. Knight for "There's nothing as sweet...." Copyright © 2004 by Linda E. Knight. All rights reserved.

A careful effort has been made to trace the ownership of selections used in this anthology in order to obtain permission to reprint copyrighted material and give proper credit to the copyright owners. If any error or omission has occurred, it is completely inadvertent, and we would like to make corrections in future editions provided that written notification is made to the publisher:

BLUE MOUNTAIN ARTS, INC., P.O. Box 4549, Boulder, Colorado 80306.